A Note to Parents

DK READERS is a compelling program for beginning readers, designed in conjunction with leading literacy experts, including Dr. Linda Gambrell, Professor of Education at Clemson University. Dr. Gambrell has served as President of the National Reading Conference, the College Reading Association, and the International Reading Association.

The DK ReaderActives line provides action-oriented illustrations, colorful page designs, and stories in which children get to make their own choices. Multiple story paths encourage children to reread their adventures to explore every possible ending. Each DK ReaderActive is guaranteed to capture a child's interest while developing his or her reading skills, general knowledge, and love of reading.

Unlike DK READERS, DK ReaderActives are not assigned a specific reading level. Generally, DK ReaderActives are best suited to Levels 2 and 3 in the list below. Younger children will surely enjoy making the story's choices while adults read aloud to them. Likewise, older children will appreciate picking their own path and trying new options with each reading.

Pre-level 1: Learning to read

Level 1: Beginning to read

Level 2: Beginning to read alone

Level 3: Reading alone

Level 4: Proficient readers

The "normal" age at which a child begins to read can be anywhere from three to eight years old. Adult participation through the lower levels is very helpful for providing encouragement, discussing storylines, and sounding out unfamiliar words. No matter which ReaderActive title you select, you can be sure that you are helping your child learn to read interactively!

DK

LONDON, NEW YORK, MUNICH,
MELBOURNE, and DELHI

For DK/BradyGames

Global Strategy Guide Publisher
Mike Degler

Licensing Manager
Christian Sumner

Editor-In-Chief
H. Leigh Davis

Operations Manager
Stacey Beheler

Title Manager
Tim Fitzpatrick

Book Designer
Tim Amrhein

Production Designer
Wil Cruz

Reading Consultant
Linda B. Gambrell, Ph.D.

A catalog record for this book is available from the Library of Congress.

ISBN: 978-0-7566-712... (...back)

Printed and bound by L... ...turing, Inc.

Nacrene City Adventures!

Written by Simcha Whitehill

DK Publishing

HOW TO USE THIS READERACTIVE

Welcome to this Pokémon ReaderActive, where *you* decide how the story unfolds! As you read, you'll find instructions at the bottom of each section of the story. These instructions fall into three categories:

1. Some instructions tell you to skip to a certain page—they look like this:

> To head straight for the famous Nacrene City Museum to check out the ancient armor, go to **PAGE 33**.

When you see an instruction like this, simply turn to the page that's listed and continue reading.

2. Other instructions let you make a choice. This is how you decide where the story takes you! Each of your options is described in its own bar, like this:

> To start with Leaf Tornado, go to **PAGE 25, TOP**.

> To use Wrap, go to **PAGE 62**.

Whichever option you choose, just skip to the listed page and continue reading. In the example above, let's say you decide to choose the first option. In that case, just turn to **PAGE 25**. Notice that the instruction also tells you to read the **TOP** entry. Sometimes instructions tell you to read the **TOP** or the **BOTTOM** of a certain page. Pay attention to this—when you turn to such a page, you'll see that the entries are marked with the words "TOP" and "BOTTOM," like this:

> **TOP**

> **BOTTOM**

Just be sure to read the right entry for your choice!

3. Every now and then, you'll reach a part of the story that is decided by chance. This is called a "Challenge." Most of the time, you'll flip a coin to determine the outcome. Here's what a Challenge section looks like:

CHALLENGE!

Flip a coin and use the results to determine your path.

 HEADS
If you land on heads, head to **PAGE 16, TOP**.

 TAILS
For tails, proceed to **PAGE 53**.

Depending on whether you get "heads" or "tails," simply turn to the indicated page and resume reading. In the example above, let's say you flip a coin and get "tails." In that case, turn to **PAGE 53** and continue the story.

That's all there is to it! Don't forget—when you finish one story, you can start over, make different choices, and create a whole new adventure! Now it's time to explore Nacrene City—have fun!

WELCOME TO NACRENE CITY!

Many talented artists, from musicians to painters, call Nacrene City home. That's why it is known for being the stylish center of the Unova region. Some even say there's a beat to the way people walk on the street. The energy of this creative city oozes with wonder because there's excitement around every colorful corner!

If you're ready to get in on all the fun, turn the page…

So, the question is: How would you like to explore this terrific town? There is so much to do, and so little time!

To travel through the city, riding around on your skateboard, go to **PAGE 12**.

To head straight for the famous Nacrene City Museum to check out the ancient armor, go to **PAGE 33**.

Or, if you're hungry, you can taste the best this town has to offer! To chow down at a local café, turn to **PAGE 20**.

"Sniiiiiivy!" it yelps, releasing its vines in Wrap.

It gets a grip on Dwebble's stone, but the Pokémon slips out from underneath it. Dwebble then scurries away.

"This is probably how it lost its last rock home," you guess. "Thanks for trying, Snivy!"

Just as you and Snivy get back on the skateboard, Dwebble quickly hops into its new stone home. Then it races straight back into the woods again.

"Look at it go!" you say. "Even though we didn't get to catch Dwebble, I'm glad we got to help it."

"Snivy!" it agrees.

You head back out toward Nacrene City, ready to meet some more Pokémon friends!

THE END

Mr. Frobro and Drilbur greet you at the quarry. You tell them you're here to find Dwebble a new stone home.

"Help yourself," Mr. Frobro generously offers.

Dwebble picks out a shiny, black stone.

"Drilburrrrr!" Drilbur yelps, clawing off a chunk for its new friend.

Dwebble then uses its saliva to melt a hole in the rock.

"Dwebble dweb!" it says, happy to have a new stone home.

You thank Drilbur and Mr. Frobro. Then you, Snivy, and Dwebble head back to town so Dwebble can use its special spit to repair all the sculptures in which it melted holes.

"Catching a Pokémon pal and saving public art— we've had an incredible first day in Nacrene City!" you say.

"Snivy!" it agrees.

THE END

You run and ask a security guard to come help the lost girl. However, by the time you get back, the girl is gone, but you and the guard find someone who looks just like you in her place!

"What's going on here?" the security guard asks.

"I don't know, I don't have a twin!" you say. "Axew, tickle the imposter to coax the person into dropping this trick!"

However, Axew is confused. It can't tell which one is the real you.

If you want to instruct Axew to tickle both you and your twin, hoping it'll reveal your identities, go to **PAGE 32**.

If you think you can help Axew figure out the faker, go to **PAGE 19**.

"Zoruaaaaaaa!" it cries.

Axew goes to see what is wrong. When it gets close, Zorua surprises it with Fury Swipes. The Tricky Fox Pokémon is an excellent actor. It has convincing Fake Tears!

"Axew, use Dragon Rage!" you instruct.

Axew shoots a big ball of light, but Zorua dodges it.

"Add Torment," Bronwyn says, smartly stopping Axew from using Dragon Rage again. Zorua then lunges its front legs forward with Scratch to win the match.

"You give great performances in acting and in battle," you say, congratulating Zorua and Bronwyn.

You can't wait to see your new friends again, whether it's at the movies or around Nacrene City!

THE END

You step outside to a nearby park. The battle is on! You want Oshawott to make the first move.

"Oshaaaaaa!" it screams as it races toward Pignite with Tackle.

However, Pignite is too strong and it stands its ground. Oshawott is ready to make its next move and so are you!

It's time to take the **Change Challenge!**

CHALLENGE!

Flip a coin and use the results to determine your path.

 HEADS
If you land on heads, go to **PAGE 28**.

 TAILS
If you land on tails, go to **PAGE 14**.

Dwebble's New Home

"Weeeeeeee!" you cheer, riding on your skateboard with the wind in your hair.

You and your Pokémon companion Snivy spot a sculpture. It depicts Lenora, the local Gym Leader. Snivy points out that the statue has a big hole in its base.

"Maybe it's just artistic license," you explain.

Next, you check out a fountain with a big, beautiful berry sculpture. Strangely enough, it has a bunch of holes in it too.

"Okay, something weird is going on here," you tell Snivy.

"Snivy!" it agrees.

You and Snivy want to solve this mystery!

To sniff out some clues around the statue, go to **PAGE 27**.

To wait at another statue and try to catch the culprit red-handed, proceed to **PAGE 38**.

"What is going on?" you ask a security guard.

"I've never seen anything so strange," the guard admits.

He tells you that the security video has him seeing double—well, twins to be exact. Every time the alarm is triggered, the video shows a pair of twins. However, each time it happens, it's a different set of twins in a different room in the museum. Also, one of the twins is always giggling.

"Giggling!" you say, putting the pieces together.

You tell the guard all about the girl you met who did nothing but giggle. "It probably isn't really a girl; it must be a shape-shifting Pokémon!" you guess.

Now, you are on the case.

Follow that giggle and continue to **PAGE 17**.

"Oshaaaaa!" it shouts, spraying Water Gun.

"Now add Tackle!" you instruct.

What a clever combination! With the ground wet from Water Gun, Pignite can't hold its ground during Tackle.

"Pig, pig, pignite!" it yells as it slips in the slippery puddle.

Oshawott then takes out its scalchop and wins the battle with a slashing Razor Shell attack.

"Congratulations!" Mrs. Sims says.

She is so impressed with your moves that she offers to take you on a tour of her super cool glass studio.

To go with Mrs. Sims, go to **PAGE 39**.

If you'd rather finally get that bite to eat, proceed to **PAGE 60**.

14

When the security guard realizes it's the famous acting team of Bronwyn and Zorua, he is so excited.

"Oh, excuse me, Miss Bronwyn. I didn't realize it was you," he apologizes.

"Quite all right, we cause a scene wherever we go. Get it, *scene*?!" she says, laughing at her own joke. "But actually, we were just leaving. Zorua and I were hoping to spend some more time practicing with our new friends."

"Sure! Axew and I are always ready for a battle," you reply.

"Axew!" it cheers. You all head to the park.

If you want to start by making the first move, go to **PAGE 54**.

To see what Zorua will do first, go to **PAGE 10**.

15

Congratulations, you are now the proud Trainer of Dwebble!

"I couldn't have done it without you, Snivy!" you say.

"Snivy!" it cheers, excited to have a new friend.

THE END

Why waste any time? You really want to catch your new friend Dwebble.

"Snivy!" your Grass-type Pokémon says, ready to battle.

"Dwebble!" your opponent says, excited.

To have Snivy start the battle with Leer, go to **PAGE 46**.

To begin with Wrap, go to **PAGE 7**.

You listen closely and hear a faint giggle coming from the next room.

"This way," you whisper.

You and Axew tiptoe over to sneak up on the girl. Then you scan her with your Pokédex. It's Zorua, the Tricky Fox Pokémon.

"Axew!" your Dragon-type Pokémon says, ready to battle.

Zorua hears Axew and now it's looking straight at you. You have to act fast!

To have Axew use Dragon Rage, go to **PAGE 45**.

To have Axew start with Scratch, go to **PAGE 30**.

You try to talk to Pignite, but it can't hear you over its own commotion. Then suddenly, you both hear a loud whistle. Pignite freezes.

"Oh, Pignite!" its Trainer, Lars, says, looking around the kitchen.

Lars explains that his Fire- and Fighting-type Pignite just lost a battle to Water-type Panpour. It took the loss pretty hard and has been feeling down ever since.

"Pignittte," it sighs.

They're about to have a rematch with Panpour, and Pignite feels pressure to prove itself. It has been chowing down to charge up for the match.

"It would be great if we could practice battle another Water-type, like your Oshawott," Lars suggests.

To battle Pignite, go to **PAGE 26**.

If you're still hungry, you can offer to cook up a special meal for everyone. Proceed to **PAGE 41**.

"Remember our first training session, Axew? You couldn't quite control Dragon Rage yet and it landed on my head," you say, laughing.

This story proves to Axew that you are its real Trainer. However, when Axew goes to give you a hug, your imposter twin sneaks in Faint Attack!

"Axew?" it says, now totally confused.

You realize you're up against a clever trickster, Zorua.

If you think things are getting a little too crazy, and you just want to put Axew back in its Poké Ball, go to **PAGE 51**.

If you still want to try to catch this shape-shifting Pokémon, go to **PAGE 57**.

Pignite's Power-Up

You and your Pokémon companion Oshawott head over to a local favorite: Yum Café. Your mouth is watering as you arrive, but when you open the door, your jaw drops. Empty food containers are everywhere and the place is a mess. It looks like a hurricane hit the restaurant—a hungry hurricane!

A Pignite is on the loose inside the restaurant. "Pignite, nite!" the Fire- and Fighting-type Pokémon yells as it approaches the refrigerator.

Food fuels the fire in Pignite's belly. When Pignite eats a lot, it gets even fiercer. Given what you see, this Pignite must be turbocharged!

"It's making such a mess," the restaurant's Chef Jebbie cries.

To have Oshawott step in and try to stop the chaos, go to **PAGE 36**.

To try to talk to Pignite and find out why it's so focused on powering up, go to **PAGE 18**.

"Drilburrrr!" a friendly Drilbur greets you at the quarry.

You explain that you're here to help Dwebble find a new home. Drilbur knows just the stone! It walks you over to a big, shiny, gray rock that sparkles in the sunlight. Drilbur uses its claws to carve out a perfect piece of the rock. Dwebble then uses its spit to melt a hole and moves into its new home.

"Dwebble!" it thanks you all with a big smile.

You have really grown to like your new friend Dwebble!

To try to catch it right in the rock quarry, go to **PAGE 16, BOTTOM**.

If you want to avoid the advantage that Dwebble, a Bug- and Rock-type Pokémon, would have at the quarry, you can head back to Nacrene City to battle. Go to **PAGE 49**.

Snivy catches Dwebble in its vines and starts to lift it away from the sculpture.

"Dwebble," it shouts, confused about what is happening.

Then, out of fear, Dwebble uses X-Scissor to free itself from Snivy's vines. It quickly scurries away.

"Sniiiiivy," Snivy sighs.

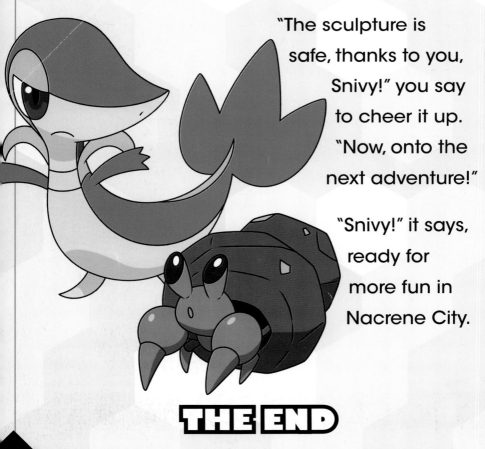

"The sculpture is safe, thanks to you, Snivy!" you say to cheer it up. "Now, onto the next adventure!"

"Snivy!" it says, ready for more fun in Nacrene City.

THE END

"This alarm is giving me a headache. I'm sorry, Axew, but we'll have to come back to the museum another day," you say.

"Axew!" it agrees.

You put Axew back in its Poké Ball to spare it from the loud noise. Then you head outside. A sculpture garden is near the museum. As you stroll by a statue of Nacrene Gym Leader Lenora, you notice there are holes at the bottom.

"Weird," you think to yourself.

Looks like you could use clever Snivy's help to solve this mystery.

Go to **PAGE 27**.

"Axewwwwwwww!" it says, unleashing its Dragon Rage attack.

The attack totally surprises Zorua. Now's your chance to catch it!

"Fingers crossed," you say, as you toss your Poké Ball.

Congratulations! You are now the proud Trainer of a Zorua.

"Thanks for all your help with Zorua!" the security guard says. "Now I need your help cleaning up this mess."

Luckily, none of the museum's art pieces got dirty, but Axew's Dragon Rage covered the floor in black soot.

"Sorry," you say to the security guard. "We'll scrub until the museum looks good as new!"

"Axew!" it agrees.

A little cleaning is a small price to pay for a sweet new Pokémon friend.

THE END

"Snivyyyyyyy!" it uses Leaf Tornado to surround Dwebble in a gust of leaves.

Dwebble is trapped in the twister. Snivy then surprises it with Tackle and knocks it over.

You toss your Poké Ball, hoping to catch your new pal.

It's time to take the **Change Challenge!**

Flip a coin and use the results to determine your path.

 HEADS
If you land on heads, go to **PAGE 16, TOP**.

TAILS
If you land on tails, go to **PAGE 53**.

"Dwebbbleeeee!" it says, backing away from Snivy's Leer.

"Way to go, Snivy!" you say.

The sculpture is safe, for now. However, you have to act quickly and make your next move.

If you and Snivy want to find a new rock home for Dwebble, so it won't keep trying to move into works of art, go to **PAGE 48**.

To have Snivy start the battle to catch Dwebble by adding Wrap, go to **PAGE 43, BOTTOM**.

"Pignite!" it shouts, ready to battle.

"Okay, Pignite, use Flame Charge!" Lars instructs the first move.

To have Oshawott boldly try to put out the flame with a splash of Water Gun, go to **PAGE 52**.

To have Oshawott try to dodge the fireball, go to **PAGE 58**.

On the ground, you find little rocks made of the same stone as the sculpture.

"These holes were drilled right here," you realize.

"Sniiiiiivy sni," Snivy says, drawing your attention to some pointy footprints.

"Good eye, Snivy! But who would leave four pointy tracks and drill rubble?" you think.
Then it hits you, "Dwebble!"

Dwebble can melt and repair rock with its special saliva. It also has a stone shell on its back, so this must be the work of a Dwebble who needs a new rock home. "Good thing the sculptures are too heavy for it to drag away!" you observe.

"Snivy!" it agrees.

You and Snivy decide you want help out the homeless Pokémon.

To ask a local sculptor to carve Dwebble a new home,
go to **PAGE 56**.

To find a suitable stone in the woods, go to **PAGE 59**.

"Osha, osha, osha," Oshawott says, trying to distract Pignite with Tail Whip.

"Pigniiiiite!" it says as it races toward Oshawott in a fiery Flame Charge.

"Dodge it!" you shout.

Oshawott doesn't move fast enough to get out of Pignite's path.

"Oshaaaa," it says, worn out.

Pignite is so strong that it has won the battle after a single move. Like a good sport, you congratulate Mrs. Sims and Pignite.

"I'm proud of you, Oshawott! You were brave to help out Chef Jebbie," you say.

You then say goodbye to your new friends. It's time to head over to the Pokémon Center so Oshawott can get a well-deserved rest.

THE END

"Axew, use Scratch!"
you command.

Before Axew can raise a claw, Zorua
surprises it with Fury Swipes.

"Zor, zor, zor!" it says, getting up in Axew's face.

Since Axew is in such close range, you could use a mean-looking
Scary Face next and go to **PAGE 42**.

Or, to have Axew blast out a powerful Dragon Rage,
go to **PAGE 24**.

"Ax, ax, ax, ax!" Axew says, swiping Zorua with Scratch.

"All right, Axew! Now add Leer," you instruct.

"Zoruaaaaaaaa," Zorua says, stunned.

While it's caught in Axew's gaze, you think fast and toss your Poké Ball, hoping to catch it.

Continue to **PAGE 35**.

Before Oshawott can distract Pignite with Tail Whip, it gets caught by something else—its Trainer.

"Pignite, what have you done?" says Mrs. Sims, Pignite's Trainer and a famous local glass artist. Then she turns to Chef Jebbie and adds, "When I heard a loud chewing noise coming from your café, I knew it must be Pignite. I'm so sorry!" "Pignite, nite," it says, to show that it's sorry.

"Actually, I could really use Pignite to perfect my flambé dessert dish," Chef Jebbie suggests.

"Pignite!" it says, excited to use its skills for cooking.

They invite you and Oshawott to stick around and try the first taste. Soon, Chef Jebbie and Pignite present you with a perfectly crispy crème brûlée.

"Delicious!" you say, digging in. "Oshawooooott," it agrees.

Everyone is happy Pignite found such a savory way to use its fire.

THE END

"Ax, ax, ax!" Axew says, tickling you.

"Ok, enough!" you giggle.

Now it's your twin's turn. The minute Axew's paws touch the faker, it turns into the Tricky Fox Pokémon, Zorua. The jig is up.

"Zorua," it shrugs.

You want to catch this amazing, shape-shifting Pokémon. So, it's time to snap into action.

Turn to **PAGE 29**.

Zorua: In Any Shape or Form

You and your Pokémon companion Axew can't wait to check out all the awesome artifacts at the Nacrene City Museum. Just as you enter, you see an entire hallway of ancient armor!

"Whoa! Looks like this one could even stop a sword," you say, pointing out a dent in the metal.

"Tee hee hee," a girl giggles next to you. Then she bends over and tries to play with Axew.

"Um, it's not a good idea to mess around in the museum," you say.

"Tee hee hee!" she giggles again.

You think this girl is acting weird. Maybe she's just being silly or maybe she's just lost.

To run and find a security guard to help her, go to **PAGE 9**.

If you want to continue making your way through the museum, go to **PAGE 47**.

"Ooooosha," Oshawott says, getting ready to blast Water Gun. However, just before Oshawott soaks Pignite, a woman with short, brown hair comes running into the café.

"Wait!" Mrs. Sims, a local glass blower, shouts.

She explains that Pignite helps her sculpt her work with its fiery moves. However, after they were offered their first big gallery show today, Pignite mysteriously disappeared.

"Pignite must be in a feeding frenzy to fire up for all the work we have to do," she said.

"Piiiiignite," it says, apologizing.

"It's okay. It's nice to know someone loves my cooking!" Chef Jebbie replies.

Since Pignite needs to blow off some steam and Oshawott still looks ready to shoot off its Water Gun attack, Mrs. Sims offers to battle you.

To decline because Pignite has an advantage now that it is charged up, go to **PAGE 63**.

To accept the challenge, go to **PAGE 11**.

Congratulations! You are now the proud Trainer of a Zorua.

"Awesome!" you cheer. "I couldn't have done it without Axew!"

"Thanks for all your help," the security guard offers. "You and Axew are a great team. Training that troublemaking Zorua will really put you to the test," the guard jokes.

"We're always up for a challenge," you reply. "Right Axew?"

"Axew!" it cheers.

THE END

"Oshawott!" it says, ready to stop Pignite's single-minded rampage.

"All right, buddy! Let's do it," you agree.

"Oh, thank you!" Chef Jebbie says.

A little strategy can go a long way in a situation like this...

To have Oshawott jump in with a big blast of Water Gun, go to **PAGE 34**.

To have Oshawott use Tail Whip to distract Pignite, go to **PAGE 31**.

Dante doesn't have time to carve something special for Dwebble because he's working on a big sculpture for the mayor. "However, you can bring Dwebble over to pick something out from my studio," Dante offers.

"Will do!" you say, thanking Dante.

You and Snivy look around town for Dwebble. Snivy spots it resting under a tree. You offer to take it to Dante's so it can pick out a new home.

"Dwebble!" it says, excited.

Together, you look through the awesome sculptures in Dante's studio. Dwebble picks out one that looks a little bit like a miniature mountain. It uses the liquid in its mouth to melt a perfect hole, and then it hops into its new home.

"Looking good, Dwebble!" you cheer.

Dwebble is so happy, but Dante seems even happier to have his piece become a walking work of art.

THE END

You and Snivy decide to stake out an untouched sculpture of a giant Poké Ball in the park. From behind a bush, Snivy spots Dwebble eyeing the big, round stone.

"Snivy," it says, ready to step in.

You have to think fast before Dwebble turns that piece of art into its new home.

To have Snivy snap into action and battle Dwebble,
go to **PAGE 43, TOP**.

If you'd rather offer to help Dwebble find a new home that isn't a public piece of art, go to **PAGE 50**.

"I'm so excited to show you how we make glass art," Mrs. Sims says, welcoming you into her studio.

"Pigniiiiiiiite!" Pignite yells, blowing a sharp flame.

Mrs. Sims holds a long, metal tube with a ball of glass on the end. She heats it in Pignite's fire. The glass is so hot, it turns a bright orange. Then, while the glass is soft, Mrs. Sims quickly uses metal tools to sculpt a blue box.

"Wow!" you say, watching her go.

"It's a gift for you, a trophy case. It can display all the Gym badges a great Trainer like you will win!" Mrs. Sims says.

You thank Mrs. Sims for the awesome present. Now you're even more excited to challenge Lenora at the Nacrene City Gym. You might earn the Basic Badge and then be able to show it off it in your new display case!

THE END

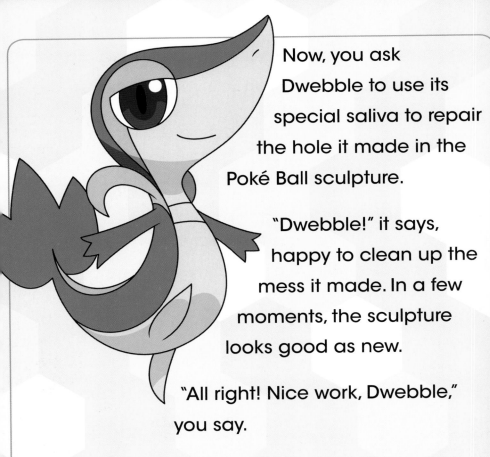

Now, you ask Dwebble to use its special saliva to repair the hole it made in the Poké Ball sculpture.

"Dwebble!" it says, happy to clean up the mess it made. In a few moments, the sculpture looks good as new.

"All right! Nice work, Dwebble," you say.

However, Dwebble has already run off to fix the other statues. While you might not have gotten the chance to catch your new friend, you're glad it's off doing the right thing.

"Snivy!" it says, hopping back onto the skateboard. You're both ready to explore more of Nacrene City!

THE END

You and the restaurant's Chef Jebbie whip up a delicious meal. It's full of good stuff, like fruits and vegetables. These will make *everyone* stronger, not just Pignite! When it's ready, you all gather around the table to dig in.

"Delicious!" Lars cheers.

"Pignite!" it agrees.

After the tasty meal, Oshawott washes the dishes using a splash of Water Gun. Pignite then dries the dishes by adding some heat with Ember. You say goodbye to your new friends, hoping your paths will cross again soon—and hopefully near a kitchen!

THE END

While Axew prepares its Scary Face move, you hear *vroom-vrrrrrrooom!* It must be Officer Jenny pulling up on her motorcycle.

"Zorua!" it says, speeding out of the museum in a flash before you can catch it.

You try to follow it into the crowded city, but Zorua has changed shapes again.

"Axew?" your Pokémon says, wondering where Zorua went.

"Zorua are slippery," says Officer Jenny. "Thanks for all your help. I can take it from here," she continues. Then she rides off to track down Zorua.

You wish you could have caught Zorua, but you sure learned that this Tricky Fox Pokémon has a lot of tricks up its sleeve. Next time you meet one, you'll be ready!

THE END

You and Snivy have decided to act fast before Dwebble zaps another sculpture.

"Snivy," it says, ready for your instructions.

To have Snivy use its vines to move Dwebble away from the Poké Ball sculpture, go to **PAGE 22**.

If you want Snivy to use Leer to lower Dwebble's defense, go to **PAGE 25, BOTTOM**.

"Snivy sniv!" Snivy says, catching Dwebble with Wrap.

You think fast and toss a Poké Ball—it works!

"Snivy!" it congratulates you on catching your new Pokémon pal, Dwebble.

"I couldn't have done it without you," you thank Snivy. "Now let's head to the rock quarry to help our friend Dwebble pick out a new rock."

Continue to **PAGE 8**

Dante welcomes you into his special sculpture studio. He shows you how to use a hammer and a chisel to shape a piece of rock. With a little hard work, you carve an awesome new stone home.

"Nice work!" Dante congratulates you with a pat on the back. "You know, I'm looking for an assistant if you're interested."

You thank Dante for the offer and all of his help, but you've got one thing on your mind right now: Dwebble! So, you and Snivy return to the sculpture of Lenora to search for Dwebble.

"Snivy!" it says, proudly pointing to Dwebble's tracks in the ground. You follow its footprints through the park until you find Dwebble. "All right, now's our big chance to try to catch it," you tell Snivy.

How do you want to kick off the battle to catch Dwebble?

To start with Leaf Tornado, go to **PAGE 25, TOP**.

To use Wrap, go to **PAGE 62**.

Zorua dodges Axew's Dragon Rage. The fireball barely misses a priceless painting, but it leaves a big blast of black ash on the wall. Zorua dashes out the door through the smoke cloud.

"Oh no! I'm so sorry," you say to the security guard. "I was just trying to help, but a museum isn't a good place to battle. Don't worry; we'll clean up the mess!"

"Axew!" your Pokémon buddy promises.

You and Axew scrub and scrub until the wall looks good as new.

"Even if your method was a little off, I'm glad you got rid of our alarm problem," the security guard says, thanking you.

THE END

"Dweebbbbblllllle," it says, intimidated by Snivy's Leer.

Then, Snivy traps Dwebble in a swirling storm of Leaf Tornado. Now, it's time to toss your Poké Ball! Your aim must be perfect. You squint to focus your eyes on the prize. You can feel a bead of sweat nervously making its way down your forehead. You toss the Poké Ball straight to Dwebble's feet. It's a perfect shot. You have caught your new friend Dwebble!

"All right!" you cheer. "I couldn't have done it without you, Snivy."

"Snivy sniv!" it says, giving you a high five.

THE END

You walk away from the armor and the strange girl. Suddenly, the museum alarm sounds. You look around the room and notice that the girl is gone.

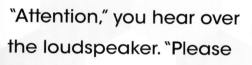

"Attention," you hear over the loudspeaker. "Please excuse the noise; we're having issues with the alarm today. We're working fast to fix it!"

"Something weird is going on at the museum today," you shout over the ringing alarm.

"Axew!" it agrees.

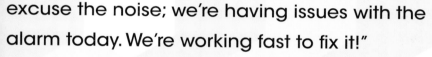

If you want to avoid the alarm noise and leave the museum, go to **PAGE 23**.

If you want to stick around to help solve the alarm problem, go to **PAGE 13**.

You and Snivy rush back with a nice rock you picked out. However, Dwebble has already made a hole and crawled into the big Poké Ball sculpture. There's a new problem: the sculpture is too heavy and now Dwebble is trapped under it.

"Snivy, use Leaf Tornado to lift it!" you suggest.

"Sniiiiiivvvvvvvy!" it yells, unleashing a strong windstorm.

The twister spins around the sculpture and picks it up just long enough for Dwebble to crawl out.

"Dweb dweb!" Dwebble says, thanking you for rescuing it.

"Why don't you try on this rock for size," you say, giving it the stone you carried over.

Dwebble melts a hole using its special saliva, and it's a perfect fit!

Continue to **PAGE 40**.

You're about to leave the quarry when you hear, "Wait!" A tall man with a big beard comes running over. It's Mr. Frobro, the owner of the quarry.

"I could really use a rock expert like you, Dwebble," he says. "Want to stay here with us?"

"Dwebble dweb," it cheers.

Even though you wish you could have caught it, you're happy you got to help the homeless Dwebble find a place to live and a new family here at the quarry!

"Take care, buddy!" you say to Dwebble.

"Dweb dwebble," it says, thanking you and Snivy for all your help.

THE END

Dwebble is just about to melt the stone with its saliva. So, you jump up from behind the bush and say, "Wait, Dwebble! Snivy and I noticed you could use a new home. We'd like to take you to the rock quarry where you can have your pick of stones!"

"Dwebble?" it says in disbelief.

"Snivy!" it promises.

The homeless Dwebble is touched that you and Snivy have offered to help it. Dwebble hops onto your skateboard for a ride to the quarry.

Continue to **PAGE 21**.

Just as you and Axew are about to leave, you hear, "I'm so sorry we bothered you!"

You turn to see a short blonde with the shape-shifting Pokémon Zorua by her side.

"Hi, I'm Bronwyn and this is my acting partner, Zorua. We've been studying new characters for our next big movie," she explains. "I guess Zorua got carried away practicing!"

"Ah, that explains a lot," you say, relieved.

"Wow, it's the famous Bronwyn!" the security guard shouts.

A crowd of people surround Bronwyn and Zorua, asking for their autographs. It looks like you've been imitated by the best—a Nacrene City celebrity! Maybe you'll turn up as a character in her next film. Wouldn't that be cool! For now, you're ready to continue looking for more adventures.

THE END

"Ossssshhhhhaaaaaa!" Oshawott says, soaking Pignite with a wave of Water Gun. No matter what fiery move Pignite was trying to use, Oshawott put out the flame.

"Pig, pig, pig, pig," Pignite huffs, out of breath.

Oshawott adds Razor Shell. With a few swipes of its scalchop, it wins the round.

"Thank you for the practice! I really learned a lot," Lars says. "When we're battling a Water-type, I need to focus on Pignite's moves that don't use fire."

"Sounds like a good strategy!" you reply.

You and Oshawott wish your new friends good luck and continue on your journey.

"Hope to run into you again soon!" Lars says, waving goodbye.

Dwebble jumps up and dodges your Poké Ball.

"Wow, look at it go!" you say, impressed that Dwebble is already able to move so quickly in its new stone home.

You might not have caught the amazing Pokémon, but you feel good that you could help a friend in need.

"Ready for more adventures in Nacrene City?" you ask Snivy.

"Snivy!" it says excitedly as you get back on your skateboard to travel through town.

THE END

"Axew, use Dragon Claw!" you command.

As Axew prepares to make its move, Zorua stops it with the steely force of its Leer move.

"Oh no, Axew!" you shout, trying to wake it up from the trance.

"Quick, add Fury Swipes!" Bronwyn tells Zorua.

However, that move actually snaps Axew back into the battle. It uses Dragon Rage to fire off a ball of energy.

"Axew, ax, ax!" it says, adding Dual Chop. You and Axew have outwitted the Tricky Fox Pokémon and won the battle!

"Congratulations! You two are a great team," Bronwyn says, impressed.

"It takes one to know one," you reply, shaking her hand.

THE END

You and Snivy find Dwebble in the park and present it with the rock. The Bug- and Rock-type pokes a hole and immediately slides into the stone.

"Hope you like it!" you say.

"Dwebble dweb dweb!" it cheers.

"Hooray!" you say, happy to help a Pokémon in need. "Dwebble, Snivy, and I would really like to add you to our team."

"Snivy!" your Pokémon companion agrees, encouraging Dwebble to join you.

To start the battle to catch Dwebble by having Snivy use Leaf Tornado, go to **PAGE 25, TOP**.

To use Wrap, go to **PAGE 62**.

You decide to visit Dante, the sculptor who carved that awesome statue of Lenora.

"Fingers crossed he'll help us help Dwebble," you hope.

You knock on the door with a *tap tap.* A cool, shaggy-haired guy in a blue-striped shirt answers.

"Hey folks, what can I do for you?" he asks.

You explain the homeless Dwebble's situation to Dante.

"Bummer! How can I help?" Dante offers.

To ask Dante to for one of his sculptures to give to Dwebble, go to **PAGE 37**.

To ask Dante to teach you how to carve Dwebble a new home, go to **PAGE 44**.

Before you and Axew get to make your move, a petite blonde woman approaches, clapping.

"Hi, I'm Bronwyn, the world-famous actress," she says, taking off her sunglasses. "I must say, you really inspired Zorua! I've never seen it so committed to playing a character."

"Thank you," you say politely. "Acting is fun...even when I don't know I'm doing it."

Just then, a security guard comes running up to your group. "Stay right there!" he shouts.

Continue to **PAGE 15**.

Oshawott dodges Pignite's Flame Charge.

"All right! Now, use Razor Shell," you shout.

Before Oshawott can grab its scalchop, Pignite cooks it with a hot Ember attack. You think fast and tell Oshawott to use Tail Whip to reduce the power of Pignite's defense.

"Pigniiiiiite!" it shouts, firing off another Flame Charge.

With that blast, Oshawott is unable to battle.

"Thank you for helping us prepare for our rematch with Panpour. I think Pignite has its battle groove back!" Lars says.

"Pignite!" it cheers.

"Good luck to you, Lars! I hope our paths cross again," you add.

"When they do, we'll be ready for a rematch!" Lars says, shaking your hand.

You and Snivy speed toward the woods on your skateboard. You both want to pick out the perfect rock. It has to be just right...

"Snivy," it says, pointing to a jagged, dome-shaped stone along the pathway.

You stop and take a look. "That's a keeper!" you agree.

Snivy helps you lift the rock up onto the skateboard. Together, you push it back into town. Now, you must find Dwebble and present your rock gift to it!

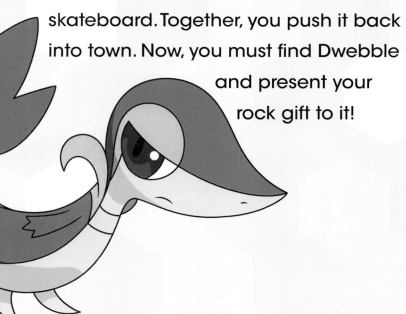

To look for Dwebble by following the footprints near the sculpture of Gym Leader Lenora, go to **PAGE 55**.

To search for Dwebble by following the footprints leading from the fountain, go to **PAGE 61**.

Grumble grumble, you hear Oshawott's belly say.

You thank Mrs. Sims for her generous offer, but it's clearly lunch time! Then you head toward the Yum Café again.

"Welcome back," Chef Jebbie says with a smile. "Order what you will; there will be no bill for my heroes!"

She shows you to a special table with a candle on it.

"Delicious!" you declare, slurping some noodles.

"Osha!" it agrees, taking a bite of berry pie.

Being helpful always makes you feel good, but this time it's particularly sweet!

THE END

You and Snivy follow the footprints from the fountain to find Dwebble huddled up in a home of leaves.

"Snivy sniv," it says, offering the rock to Dwebble.

Dwebble crawls out of the leaves with a big smile on its face.

"Dwebble dweb dweb!" it says, thanking you.

Using the special saliva from its mouth, Dwebble melts a hole in the rock, then another, and another, and so on. Soon, Dwebble has a polka-dot patterned home.

"So cool!" you applaud.

In this creative town, it looks like even the Pokémon are artistic!

THE END

"Sniiiivy!" it shouts, getting ready to unleash Wrap.

However, Dwebble buries Snivy with Rock Slide before it has the chance to make its move.

"Dwebble!" it says, scurrying off into the city traffic.

"Sniiii," Snivy sighs.

"We gave it our best shot," you remind Snivy. "Not only that, but we also helped a Pokémon in need. That's something we can feel good about, no matter the outcome of the battle."

You and Snivy get back on your skateboard to start another adventure.

"Thank you for the offer, but Oshawott and I are still hungry. So, we need to grab a bite to eat," you explain to Mrs. Sims.

"Yeah, and I guess Pignite and I should get started cleaning up the mess at Yum Café anyway," Mrs. Sims admits. "Well, I hope our paths cross again."

"If they do, the battle will be on!" you promise.

"Osha!" your Pokémon companion agrees.

THE END

Glossary

ancient
very old; prehistoric

artistic license
the freedom of an artist or writer to distort or ignore fact for the sake of dramatic effect

chaos
disorder; commotion; confusion

convincing
realistic; believable; persuasive

crème brûlée
a rich custard dessert that is sprinkled with sugar and placed under a broiler until a brown crust forms on top

culprit
criminal; a person who is guilty of a crime or a fault

decline
refuse; turn down; reject

depict
to represent something with words, a picture, or a sculpture

flambé
dipped in or covered with a flammable liqueur and set afire when served

generously
unselfishly; liberally; selflessly

identity
the set of traits by which a thing or person is recognized or known

imitated
copied; mimicked; impersonated

imposter
one that assumes false identity for the purpose of deception

impressed
affected strongly in mind or feelings; influenced in opinion

intimidated
scared; threatened; unsettled

petite
small; slender; trim

quarry
an open pit from which stone is obtained by digging, cutting, or blasting

rampage
violent or excited behavior that is reckless or destructive

saliva
slobber; drool; a clear, watery liquid secreted into the mouth that lubricates chewed food and begins the breakdown of starches

savory
pleasant or agreeable in taste or smell; flavorful; salty; appetizing

sculptor
one who shapes, molds, or fashions, especially with artistry; one whose occupation is to carve statues or works of sculpture

single-minded
focused; determined; strong-willed; persistent

triggered
caused; put in motion; initiated

Index